20TH CENTURY SCIENCE & TECHNOLOGY

1960s

SPACE AND TIME

20TH CENTURY SCIENCE & TECHNOLOGY – 1960s
was produced by

David West ☗ **Children's Books**
7 Princeton Court
55 Felsham Road
London SW15 1AZ

Designers: Jenny Skelly & Aarti Parmar
Editor: James Pickering
Picture Research: Brooks Krikler Research

First published in Great Britain in 2000 by
Heinemann Library, Halley Court, Jordan Hill,
Oxford OX2 8EJ, a division of Reed Educational and
Professional Publishing Limited.

OXFORD MELBOURNE AUCKLAND
JOHANNESBURG BLANTYRE GABORONE
IBADAN PORTSMOUTH (NH) USA CHICAGO

04 03 02 01 00
10 9 8 7 6 5 4 3 2 1

ISBN 0 431 12193 1 (HB)
ISBN 0 431 12200 8 (PB)

British Library Cataloguing in Publication Data

Parker, Steve, 1952 -
1960s space and time -
(Twentieth century science & technology).
1. Technology - History - 20th century -
Juvenile literature
2. Science - History - 20th century -
Juvenile literature
I. Title
609' .046

Printed and bound in Italy

PHOTO CREDITS:
Abbreviations: t-top, m-middle, b-bottom,
r-right, l-left, c-centre.

Cover - Corbis, Corbis Images. Pages 4t,
5 all, 6, 10, 10-11, 11 all, 12 both, 13t,
16-17b, 18-19m & b, 19t, 20b, 21, 22r,
24m, 24-25, 25b, 26, 27tl, 28 & 28-29 -
Corbis. 4b, 7, 16-17t, 18, 20t, 22l, 23
both, 24b, 27tr & b - Hulton Getty
Collection. 8t, 9, 12-13, 14ml & mr &
17t - Corbis Images. 8b & 18-19t -
Solution Pictures.13b - Novosti. 14t & b
- NASA. 19b, 29t & b - David West. 29m
- Science & Society.

*The dates in brackets after a person's
name give the years that he or she lived.*

*An explanation of difficult words can be
found in the glossary on page 30.*

20TH CENTURY SCIENCE & TECHNOLOGY

1960s
SPACE AND TIME

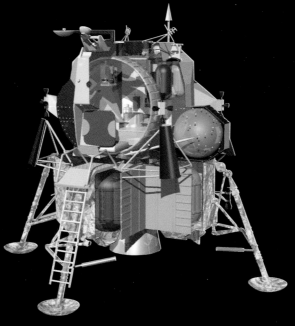

Steve Parker

Heinemann
LIBRARY

CONTENTS

1960 saw the invention of the laser – a pure, concentrated and powerful source of light. In a few years lasers had hundreds of varied applications.

THE SPACE RACE

The decade of the 1960s will always be remembered for the 'space race'. The two world superpowers of the USA and USSR (now mainly Russia/CIS) competed against each other for space firsts: to put a person into orbit around Earth, to launch more and better satellites, to build space stations, to send probes to distant planets, and perhaps the greatest achievement of all, to land astronauts on the Moon. Amazingly, all of this happened during the '60s.

However it was not just 'firsts' at stake. Each great nation also saw how space could be used for military purposes by orbiting spy satellites and missiles of mass destruction. As the decade developed, the rush for supremacy in space drove scientific research and technological invention at a great pace. Spin-offs from space and military programmes flooded into everyday life, ranging from live colour television beamed around the world by satellite, and sight-saving laser eye surgery, to plastic disposable clothes and non-stick coatings on frying pans.

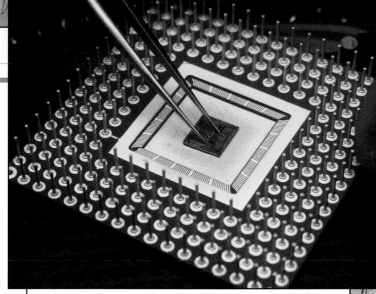

The push to make electronic circuits smaller, especially for military equipment, led to the first microchips in about 1967.

John Glenn was the third US astronaut to reach space and the first to orbit Earth, in 1962. But the USSR had already put the first person into space in 1961.

Telstar 2 was an early comsat (communications satellite), relaying phone calls and television channels.

New, cheap plastic materials encouraged bold and daring fashions like see-through throwaway dresses.

SIZE MATTERS

In the 1910s scientists split atoms, showing that these were not the smallest or most fundamental particles of matter. Atoms were made of even tinier bits, such as electrons, protons and neutrons. By the 1960s, new evidence from more powerful particle-accelerators or 'atom-smashers' pointed to even smaller particles.

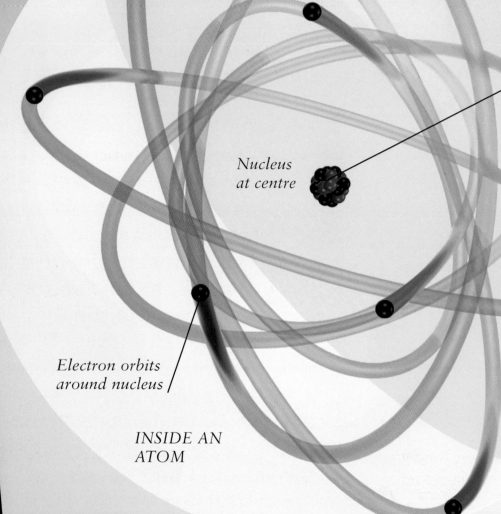

Nucleus at centre

Electron orbits around nucleus

INSIDE AN ATOM

THE QUARK

In the 1950s Murray Gell-Mann, at the California Institute of Technology, had studied cosmic rays. Strange particles in them did not follow the usual laws of atomic physics. Gell-Mann analyzed the idea of 'strangeness' using maths and extended it to the structure of the atom. In 1964 his 'eight-fold way' theory was confirmed by experiments. It showed that protons, neutrons and similar particles were in fact made of even smaller pieces – quarks.

Murray Gell-Mann (born 1929) became Professor of Theoretical Physics in 1956 and received a Nobel Prize for physics in 1969.

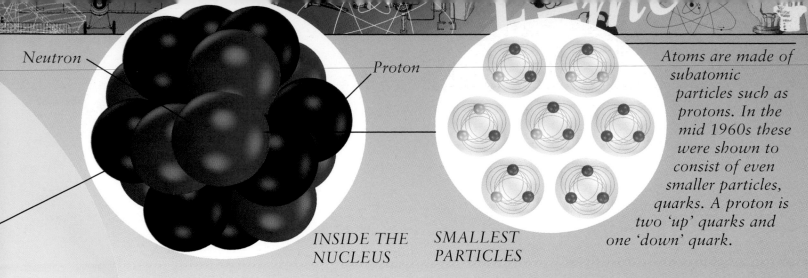

Neutron

Proton

INSIDE THE NUCLEUS

SMALLEST PARTICLES

Atoms are made of subatomic particles such as protons. In the mid 1960s these were shown to consist of even smaller particles, quarks. A proton is two 'up' quarks and one 'down' quark.

EARTH ON THE MOVE

On a larger scale, new science was solving ancient mysteries. Paleomagnetism was the developing study of particles magnetized by the Earth's natural magnetic field, trapped as rocks formed millions of years ago. It helped to show how continents had moved. With more new information, especially from the first survey satellites, it supported the idea of continental drift suggested in 1912 by German weather expert Alfred Wegener. Earth's land masses were once all together and drifted to their present positions – the theory of plate tectonics.

PLATE TECTONICS

In the 1960s new evidence from rock layers, drill holes, satellites and fossils came together into the theory of plate tectonics, often called continental drift. This says the major land masses are carried around the globe on giant curved plates of rock. The plates grow as molten rock oozes from below and adds to their edges. They crumple into mountains, and cause earthquakes and volcanoes as they rub together. Then they shrink as they are forced back into the Earth.

Alfred Wegener (1880-1930)

Rock layers crumpled into mountains

Continent movement

Seabed crust slides under continental crust

Ocean

Two seabed plates move apart

New rock wells up from below

UP THERE

As superpowers raced to launch astronauts, astronomers peered through telescopes across the Universe and analyzed the mass of information from new satellites and space probes.

RADIO ASTRONOMY

Radio telescopes detect natural radio and similar waves coming from the sky (see panel opposite). These invisible rays provide information about objects deep in space. In 1963, radio astronomers noticed an incredibly powerful source of radio and other waves far across the Universe. It seemed no bigger than an average star, like our Sun, yet gave out more energy than 100 whole galaxies. It was called a quasar. A quasar is thought to be matter and energy falling into a giant black hole at the centre of a galaxy.

A pulsar 'flashes' on and off like a lighthouse, sending out radio rather than light waves. It is a fast-spinning neutron star – the dense core of an old star which has exploded.

Some radio telescopes have many dish antennae linked by computer. They work as one giant dish to detect very weak radio signals.

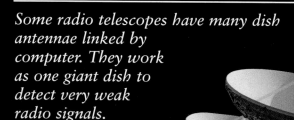

UFO FEVER

Regular radio blips from pulsars fuelled ideas of aliens in space. Might they visit Earth? Many UFOs (unidentified flying objects) were photographed and 'UFO fever' gripped the world. But some were hoaxes, some were natural weather features like ball lightning and some were secret military test craft. As far as we know, none was an alien spacecraft.

The UFO C-9, photographed in the '60s.

8

BLIP, BLIP, BLIP, BLIP

In 1967 a huge radio telescope was built at the Mullard Radio Astronomy Laboratory, Cambridge, UK. The team was led by Antony Hewish (born 1924) and included student astronomer Jocelyn Bell (born 1943). Within weeks they noticed strange, regular pulses of radio signals, 1.3 seconds apart, from far away in our Galaxy. Were they call-signs from aliens? By the end of 1967 the team found another pulsing object. They worked out the signals were given off by fast-spinning neutron stars – small, incredibly dense remnants of old giant stars that collapse into themselves. The new discoveries were called pulsars. Since the '60s many more quasars and pulsars have been identified.

A quasar pours out unimaginable amounts of energy from the heart of a galaxy. Some quasars emit mainly light, others send out radio waves. They are among the most distant and powerful objects discovered so far.

RADIO TELESCOPES

Our eyes see light rays from the Sun, Moon, stars, planets and other objects in space. But many other kinds of rays also reach Earth from space, including natural radio waves, microwaves and cosmic rays. They are invisible to our eyes but radio telescopes can 'see' or detect them. Radio telescopes use antennae (aerials) shaped like large dishes, similar to huge satellite TV dishes, or long wires strung on towers to receive the signals. Radio astronomy began in the mid 1940s but expanded greatly in the 1960s.

Parabolic dish reflects and concentrates incoming waves on to receiver

Dish tilt mechanism

Receiver

Incoming waves

Signal computing and analysis building

Dish control and radio receiver building

Support tower

THE RACE IS ON

At the beginning of the 1960s most independent experts agreed that the USA led the USSR, in space technology. It was a shock when the USSR announced it had put the first human into space, on 12 April 1961.

President Khrushchev of the USSR meets fellow communist leader Fidel Castro of Cuba in 1963.

THE COLD WAR

The Cold War was a tense stand-off between the capitalist USA and allied western nations, and the communist-based USSR and eastern European allies. The success of the first manned space flight was a huge boost for the USSR's scientific reputation and for its political system and communist friends. Its president Nikita Khrushchev welcomed the news with great pride.

During the Cold War of the 1960s, Soviet Russia frequently displayed its military might. Intercontinental ballistic missiles, armed with nuclear warheads, which could reach the other side of the world, were one spin-off from the space race.

THE FIRST TRIP INTO SPACE

Gagarin's craft, *Vostok 1*, was launched by a Soviet A-1 rocket with the aid of four strap-on boosters. The capsule itself measured 2.3 metres across and weighed 2.4 tonnes. It had very few controls – the astronaut was largely a passenger for the trip. *Vostok 1* reached a maximum height of 327 kilometres on its single-orbit journey. Its shield deflected the enormous heat of re-entry as the craft plunged back into the blanket of air around Earth, the atmosphere, at more than 8,000 km/h. A parachute slowed the final descent to the ground. At the time the USSR announced that Gagarin stayed in his craft until it landed. In fact he ejected at a height of about 6 kilometres and parachuted down separately. On 16 June 1963 *Vostok 6* carried the first woman, Valentina Tereshkova, into space.

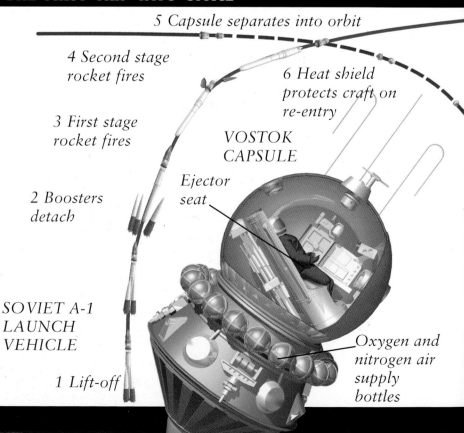

5 Capsule separates into orbit

4 Second stage rocket fires

3 First stage rocket fires

2 Boosters detach

6 Heat shield protects craft on re-entry

VOSTOK CAPSULE

Ejector seat

SOVIET A-1 LAUNCH VEHICLE

1 Lift-off

Oxygen and nitrogen air supply bottles

In 1961 President John F Kennedy declared the USA's main aim in space – to land a man on the Moon and bring him back safely by the end of the decade.

FIRST IN SPACE

The first person in space was Yuri Gagarin, a former USSR air force pilot. His craft, the ball-shaped Vostok, had already been used to carry Sputnik satellites and was tested in several unmanned flights. Gagarin took off from Baikanour Space Centre, made one orbit of Earth and landed near the Volga River after a flight lasting one hour 48 minutes.

John Glenn (born 1921) made his first flight in a Mercury craft, Friendship 7. *In 1998 he became the oldest astronaut when he went into space again on the space shuttle.*

THE USA'S REPLY

The USA was stung into action and soon had its own astronauts. Two up-and-down 'hops' were made in 1961, by Alan Shepard on 5 May and Virgil Grissom on 21 July. On the third trip John Glenn made three full Earth orbits, on 20 February 1962. The USSR now concentrated on building an orbiting space station and unmanned deep-space probes. The USA, on the other hand, developed from the one-person *Mercury* craft, to the two-person *Gemini*, then to the three-person *Apollo* – to send astronauts to the Moon.

After his space trip Gagarin (1934–68) became director of the USSR's programme to train women astronauts. He was due to return to space in a Soyuz craft when he was killed in a jet fighter training accident.

7 Gagarin ejects from re-entry capsule and lands by parachute

SATELLITE REVOLUTION

A satellite is now launched every week or two. But in the 1960s satellites were new and every launch made global headlines. Some, like *Telstar* and *Early Bird*, became almost like celebrities – as famous as the human stars of movies, sport and pop music.

HARD WORKERS

The TIROS series of 10 satellites, launched between 1960 and 1965, carried television cameras to picture the clouds far below. They also detected temperature at different heights above the ground. The information was radioed down to Earth and used to make the first satellite-aided weather forecasts.

A technician tests one of the two television cameras on TIROS 10 (Television and Infrared Observation Satellite), in 1965.

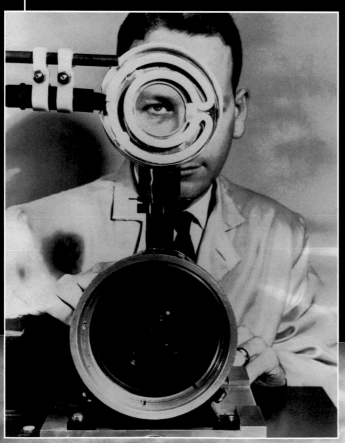

Telstar 2 *was an aluminium sphere 87 cm across weighing 79 kg. The large dark squares are solar cells to turn sunlight into electricity. The small 'spokes' in the square openings around the middle are microwave aerials.*

12

Today a small dish antenna can receive satellite TV. In the '60s huge dishes like Goonhilly in Cornwall, England picked up the signals and passed them to the usual terrestrial system.

LIVE AT LAST

Much more famous were the two *Telstar* comsats (communication satellites). In July 1962, *Telstar 1* sent live black-and-white television pictures from the USA to Europe. In May 1963, *Telstar 2* went one better and relayed the first live colour television images across the Atlantic. Because the satellites were in low oval orbits they could only be used for short periods, unlike today's television satellites.

Astronauts go on space walks when they need to repair their craft, or satellites. First was the USSR's Alexei Leonov in 1965, soon followed by the USA's Edward White, shown above.

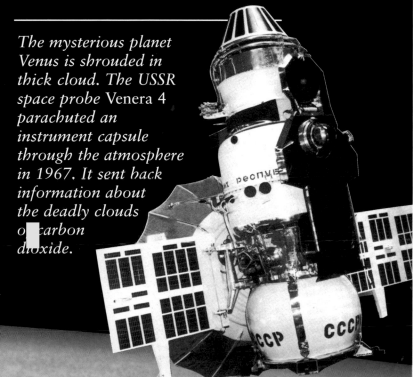

The mysterious planet Venus is shrouded in thick cloud. The USSR space probe Venera 4 parachuted an instrument capsule through the atmosphere in 1967. It sent back information about the deadly clouds of carbon dioxide.

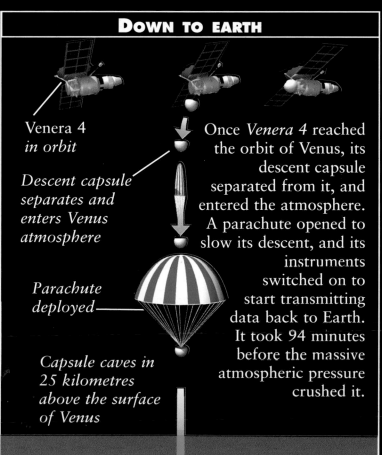

DOWN TO EARTH

Venera 4 in orbit

Descent capsule separates and enters Venus atmosphere

Parachute deployed

Capsule caves in 25 kilometres above the surface of Venus

Once *Venera 4* reached the orbit of Venus, its descent capsule separated from it, and entered the atmosphere. A parachute opened to slow its descent, and its instruments switched on to start transmitting data back to Earth. It took 94 minutes before the massive atmospheric pressure crushed it.

ON THE MOON!

The most spectacular science-based event of the 20th century happened on 20 July 1969. For the first time humans walked on another world – the Moon.

Apollo 11 *crew (from left): Neil Armstrong, Michael Collins, 'Buzz' Aldrin.*

APOLLO PROGRAMME

The Moon landing was the climax of ten years of incredible technological advance in almost all areas of science, from computing to medicine. Early unmanned *Apollo* space shots tested the vehicles and equipment. From *Apollo 7* in October '68, astronauts went too. In May '69 *Apollo 10* went all the way to the Moon and carried out all the tests, but did not land.

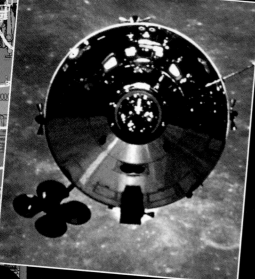

Collins in the Apollo *command module stayed in Moon orbit.*

14

The American flag is saluted on the Moon's surface, with the lunar module in the background.

THE WORLD IS AMAZED

Apollo 11 was the first Moon landing. Its commander Neil Armstrong (born 1930) stepped from the lunar module on to the grey, dusty surface with the historic words: 'That's one small step for a man, one giant leap for mankind.' They collected 25 kilograms of Moon rocks and dust. The last Moon mission was *Apollo 17* in 1972. Nobody has set foot there since.

Apollo 13 crew splash down safely in 1970. Their trip was cut short by technical failures.

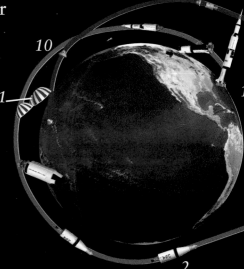

9

10

11

1

2

THE APOLLO MISSION

An *Apollo* mission had four parts. The *Saturn V* rocket was the launch vehicle. The astronauts inhabited the Command Module (CM). This was attached to the Service Module (SM) with its life-support equipment and rocket, except for final re-entry to Earth. The Lunar Module (LM) detached from the CM to land on the Moon with two astronauts. Its ascent stage took off to rejoin the CM in Moon orbit.

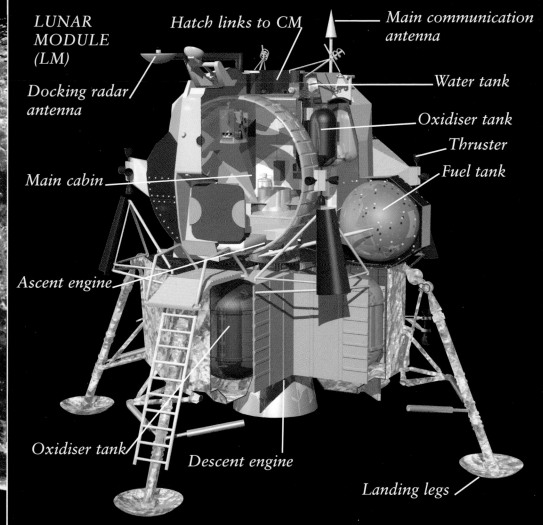

LUNAR MODULE (LM)

Hatch links to CM

Main communication antenna

Docking radar antenna

Water tank

Oxidiser tank

Thruster

Fuel tank

Main cabin

Ascent engine

Oxidiser tank

Descent engine

Landing legs

SATURN V

Escape tower

Command module

Service module

Lunar module

Third stage S-IVB

Rocket J-2 engine

Second stage S-II

5 Rocket J-2 engines

First stage SIC

5 Rocket F-1 engines

1 Launch
2 Apollo leaves Earth's orbit
3 Lunar Module (LM) docks with Command Module (CM)
4 Two day trip to the Moon
5 LM & CM enter Moon's orbit
6 LM separates from CM and lands on the Moon
7 LM leaves Moon and links up with CM
8 CM leaves lunar orbit for Earth
9 CM detatches from SM and enters Earth orbit
10 Re-entry into Earth's atmosphere
11 Splashdown

15

CUTTING EDGE

Lasers are vital in daily life. Different types are used in CD players, telephone optical fibres, holograms, medicine, cutting and welding metals, making microchips and hundreds of other things. This versatile device dates back to 1960 when US physicist Theodore Maiman powered up the first working version.

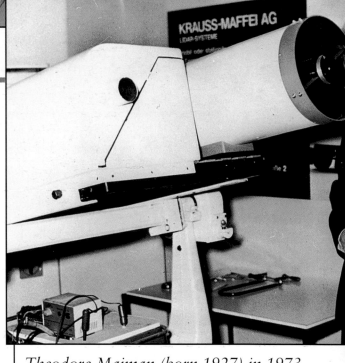

Theodore Maiman (born 1927) in 1973 with Russian scientist Alexandr Prokhorov (left). Prokhorov's research work helped Maiman to construct a practical laser.

HOW A LASER WORKS

A laser is based on a substance called the active medium – in Maiman's case, a rod of ruby crystal. A flash tube wrapped around it pumps light energy into the crystal. The energy makes atoms in the crystal give off bursts of their own light. These gather together, bounce to and fro between mirrors, become stronger and finally emerge through the partially reflecting mirror.

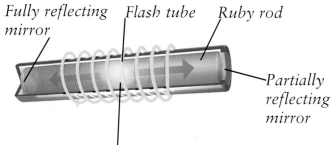

Fully reflecting mirror   Flash tube   Ruby rod

Partially reflecting mirror

Light flash from tube gives atoms extra energy

Atoms give off energy as bursts of light

Bursts build up and reflect to and fro within rod

Light escapes through partial mirror as powerful, pure, non-spreading laser beam

MASERS TO LASERS

The idea behind the laser was not new. A similar device called a maser, that works with microwaves rather than light waves, had been built in 1954. Maiman developed the research work of other scientists and applied the same process to make a powerful light beam of a pure single colour that did not spread out. Three of these other scientists received Nobel Prizes in 1964 but Maiman did not.

A scientist tries a laser using gas as the active medium. Laser light waves are all the same length, unlike ordinary light which has mixed wavelengths.

CRACKING THE CODE

Cracking the genetic code began in 1961. The genetic substances DNA and RNA have different sequences of chemicals that code for different amino acids – substances which clip together to make proteins, from which all living things are built. The first 'code-word' to be identified was the sequence UUU which represented the amino acid phenylalanine.

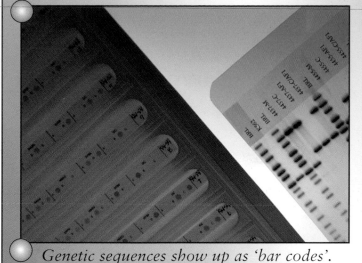

Genetic sequences show up as 'bar codes'.

LASERS EVERYWHERE

Within a year of Maiman's invention, other scientists were developing stronger and more powerful versions, and also more delicate and accurate lasers for eye surgery (see page 26). In 1965 the first holograms were produced using laser light. Holograms are images that can be viewed from different angles to see around and behind objects, yet they are contained on a flat surface.

THE HOLOGRAM

A holographic image is recorded on photographic film like an ordinary photo. But it does not show different colours and shades of light. It shows where two sets of laser light beams come together and interfere or cancel each other out. One set is direct from the laser. The other is reflected from the object.

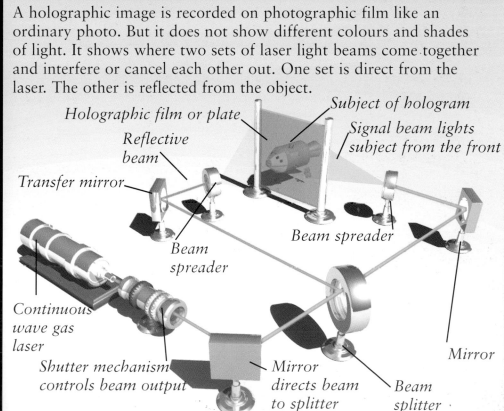

Holographic film or plate

Subject of hologram

Signal beam lights subject from the front

Reflective beam

Transfer mirror

Beam spreader

Beam spreader

Continuous wave gas laser

Shutter mechanism controls beam output

Mirror directs beam to splitter

Beam splitter

Mirror

ON THE MOVE

No major new forms of transport were invented during the 1960s. But 1969 saw the first flights of two very different aircraft. These suggested how long-distance air travel might progress in different ways. They were the Boeing 747 Jumbo jet and the joint French-English jetliner Concorde.

Boeing 747s are still in service with more than 50 airlines around the world.

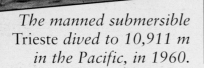

The manned submersible Trieste dived to 10,911 m in the Pacific, in 1960.

FAST VERSUS BIG

Concorde was for people with money and in a hurry. It crossed the Atlantic in about three hours, cruising at 2,170 kilometres per hour (twice the speed of sound) with about 100 passengers. But the plane encountered several problems such as the high temperatures created on its metal 'skin' by its great speed, its noisy engines, and the sonic boom as it went faster than sound. It did not enter service until 1976. The Jumbo was mainly existing technologies made bigger. It went into service in 1970, and in various models since, has sold well over 1,000 compared to Concorde's 15.

Japanese Shinkansen 'bullet trains' went into service in 1965, almost halving the journey time on some routes.

THE TURBOFAN

The Jumbo jet had a new type of jet engine, the turbofan. It was similar to a standard jet but with a very large, angle-bladed turbine 'fan' at the front. The fan worked like a propeller to push air backwards around the engine for added thrust. This 'bypass' air also made the main engine run at a lower temperature and more quietly.

Large fan provides extra thrust

Turbines drive compressor and large fan

Exhaust

Combustion chamber

Compressor fan squashes air

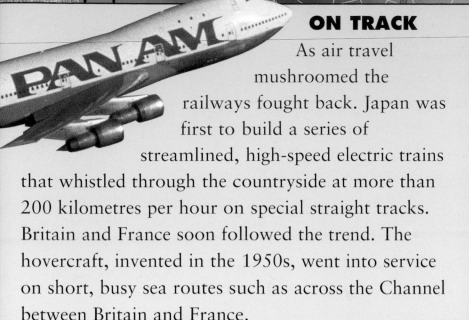

ON TRACK

As air travel mushroomed the railways fought back. Japan was first to build a series of streamlined, high-speed electric trains that whistled through the countryside at more than 200 kilometres per hour on special straight tracks. Britain and France soon followed the trend. The hovercraft, invented in the 1950s, went into service on short, busy sea routes such as across the Channel between Britain and France.

Concorde is operated by the national airlines of Britain and France. It is still the only faster-than-sound passenger craft.

THE PERSONAL JET

The Bell Company's 'Pogo' was an experimental platform thrust into the air by its own jet. It was part of a combined research programme into vertical take-off jet planes, military 'jet belts' and maybe one day, personal jet-powered hovercraft.

A Bell Pogo trip in 1967.

SMALLEST AND DEEPEST

The '60s pioneering spirit extended from space to the ground and far below. The tiny Mini car was advertised as fun to drive and convenient around town. It caught the public's imagination despite cramped seats and minimal luggage space. In 1960 Jacques Piccard and Donald Walsh descended to the deepest part of the ocean, the Marianas Trench near Japan, in the deep-sea submersible *Trieste* – still a record deep dive.

The Austin-Morris Mini was designed in 1959 by Alec Issigonis. Its transverse (crossways) engine and front wheel drive saved parts and so space and cost.

ON THE MAKE

'Unitary technology' took off in the '60s. All kinds of objects, from plastics to whole skyscrapers, were made from many identical units or modules.

HOUSES FROM FACTORIES

Inspired by the experimental spirit of the decade, architects and building engineers designed houses based on mass-produced sections or modules. These were made in factories, then quickly 'plugged in' on site. The aim was to manufacture modern, safe, hygienic housing at a very low cost.

COLLAPSE

Unitary or modular building seemed safe if all modules stayed intact to give strength to the whole structure. Then a small gas explosion in one room of the Ronan Point tower block collapsed the whole side of the building as if made from playing cards. The safety of the modular system was in doubt.

The collapse of Ronan Point, London, 1968.

MASS-PRODUCED LIVING BOXES

The modular system applied the idea of the assembly line to making entire houses, offices and factories. It seemed quick, simple and cheap. But in practice some of the materials were not strong or long-lasting enough. In certain buildings the roofs leaked, the walls and joints cracked and the floors were not level.

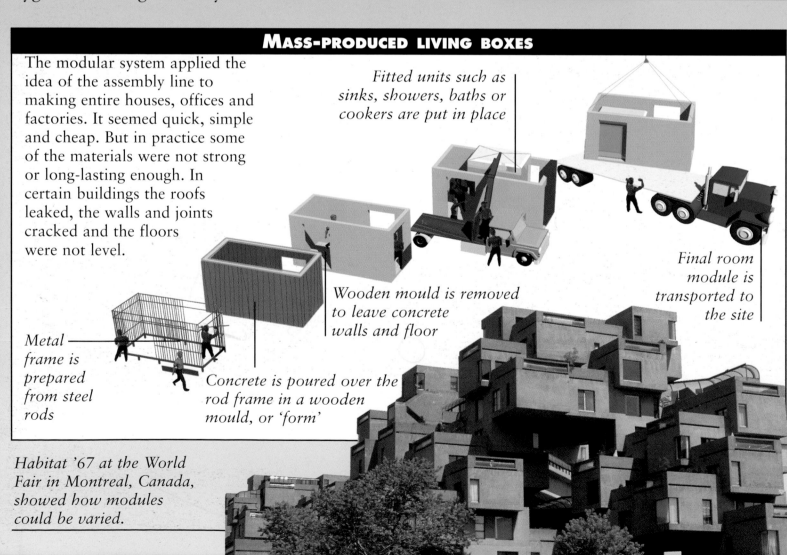

Fitted units such as sinks, showers, baths or cookers are put in place

Final room module is transported to the site

Wooden mould is removed to leave concrete walls and floor

Metal frame is prepared from steel rods

Concrete is poured over the rod frame in a wooden mould, or 'form'

Habitat '67 at the World Fair in Montreal, Canada, showed how modules could be varied.

Lake Point Tower, in Chicago, was completed in 1968. Its sleek undulating glass walls were based on sketches made in 1921 by Mies van der Rohe who proposed a curving glass curtain wall – structurally impossible at that time.

LASTING TECHNOLOGY

Modular building used new, strong plastics shaped and moulded on production lines. But many people did not want to live in 'little boxes' that were the same as everyone else's homes. A much more lasting innovation was the float glass process for making large sheets of glass quickly and cheaply. Many '60s skyscrapers look like giant slabs of glass.

FLOAT GLASS

Glass was easy to blow into bottles and similar shapes but difficult to form into large, flat sheets. The float glass process developed by the 1960s was a great leap forward. Molten or runny glass was allowed to spread over a bath of molten tin, heated to more than 230°C. The glass oozed like syrup to form a ribbon, smooth on the top and against the mirror-like surface of the tin beneath.

| Raw glass mix | Oil-fired melting furnace | Syrupy molten glass floats on tin bath | Glass ribbon is cooled in annealing lehr to make it hard and strong | Sheets are cut from glass ribbon | Sheets taken to warehouse |

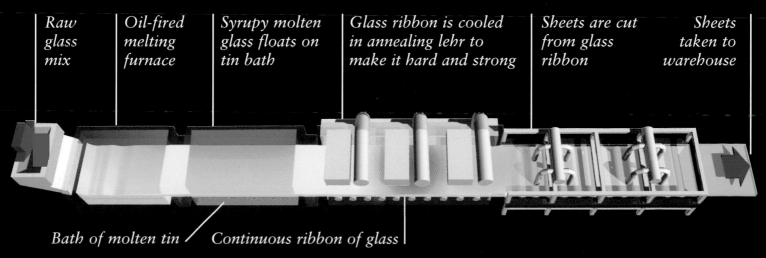

Bath of molten tin / *Continuous ribbon of glass*

THE PLASTIC AGE

As more people bought cars, and more goods were transported by road, the need for petrol and diesel fuels rose. These fuels are made from petroleum (crude oil), and some of the by-products of the process generated their own industry – plastics.

POLYMERS

Many petrochemical by-products and other substances can be broken down into what chemists call monomer hydrocarbons. These are small molecules containing only hydrogen and carbon. The monomers are then heated and treated to link them together into polymers, like beads in enormously long molecular necklaces, to produce dozens of different types of plastics.

Plastics and artificial fibres were styled in the 1960s into exciting new fashions. Here, a model is wearing a PVC coat, designed by Yves St Laurent in 1966.

22

MAKING ACRYLIC

Acrylic is the plastic polymer PMMA, polymethyl methacrylate. It can be 'squirted' through tiny holes in a spinneret to make fibres, or formed into blocks and sheets for all kinds of uses, from signs to aircraft windows.

Mix is dissolved in solvent

Raw ingredients are combined or polymerised

Impurities are filtered out

Acrylic fibre is drawn through dryer and then on to be stretched, crimped and baled

Liquid acrylic is forced through spinneret into bath to form fibre

PLASTICS EVERYWHERE

Acrylic-type plastics had first been developed in the 1930s as glass-like clear sheets. With names such as Perspex and Plexiglass they were used for high-speed or high-stress applications where glass might shatter, splinter and cause injury. In the 1960s, acrylic followed rayon and nylon to become the latest, most fashionable artificial fibre. It could be produced in bright, non-fade colours, drip-dried quickly and needed little care – ideal for the fast '60s lifestyle.

The transparent TV's Perspex case of 1960 revealed the new transistors and circuits inside.

1967's Blow Chair supposedly spread the body's weight for ultra-comfort. But a tiny pinprick…

BECAUSE THEY'RE THERE

The rush to develop new plastics and similar artificial materials led to some very unusual products, such as see-through televisions and blow-up furniture. Many of these were designed simply because now they could be. With the pioneering feel of the space race, materials technologists pushed these new substances to the limit in all manner of unusual ways.

THE THROWAWAY SOCIETY

During the 1960s most people were not yet aware of environmental concerns and the need to conserve and recycle natural resources. It was a bright, breezy decade of fast fashions and quirky ideas. The same applied to manufacturing. These transparent dresses from 1966 were made of plastic. They were uncomfortable and sticky to wear, but that mattered little. They were designed to be worn once or twice, then thrown away.

Dresses by Hechter of Paris.

ELEC-TECH

Domestic electrical equipment of the 1960s benefited greatly from the space race and military research. By 1970 transistors, in general use since the early 1950s, were already being replaced by integrated circuits.

THE MARVELLOUS CHIP

An integrated circuit, IC, is made with all the transistors, resistors and other electronic components already in position and connected together or integrated, rather than manufactured separately and linked by wires. One tiny IC or 'chip' contains thousands of such components.

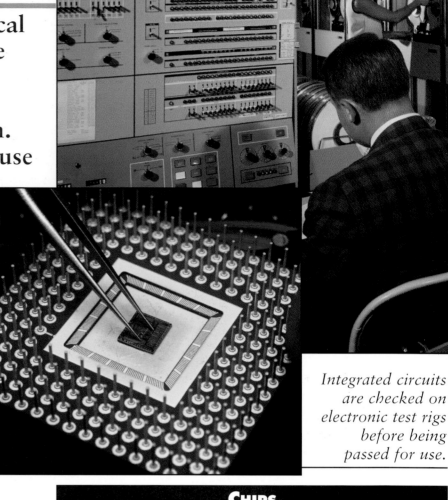

Integrated circuits are checked on electronic test rigs before being passed for use.

Radio had its own massive trade shows and exhibitions, with hundreds of models on display.

CHIPS

Integrated circuits are made from semi-conductor materials such as silicon or germanium, grown in high-pressure vats as lump crystals. Thin wafers are sliced off and cut into chips. Components are etched or 'carved' onto the surface with acid or laser light.

5 Chip incorporated into plastic case with connectors

4 Wafer cut into chips

3 Components printed or etched on wafer

1 Silicon crystal

2 Silicon wafer

24

THE COMPUTER KEY

In the early 1960s computers were rare and room-sized, found only in government departments, big businesses and universities. Gradually they were reduced to the size of filing cabinets. They were not operated directly by ordinary typewriter-style keyboards until 1967. Before this the programmes and information were fed in from reels of punched paper tape or magnetic tape. The Internet started in about 1969 as a US Department of Defence and inter-university network.

Large reels of magnetic tape dominate the IBM 360 computer room in this 1969 view of the Seabord Coast Line railroad offices, USA.

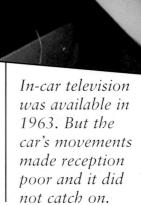

In-car television was available in 1963. But the car's movements made reception poor and it did not catch on.

CONSUMER BOOM

During the 1960s the leading industrial nations grew very wealthy, especially in North America and Europe, also Japan and Australia. People had money to spend, which encouraged new areas of manufacturing. Radios, televisions, vinyl record players and similar equipment sold in huge numbers. The 'vinyl' of the record was based on polyvinyl chloride, PVC, yet another type of plastic polymer.

Mass-pressed vinyl audio discs, called 'records', generated the new industry of popular music.

MEDICAL SCIENCE

A patient is prepared for laser eye surgery in the early 1960s.

MOne of medical history's greatest events took place in Cape Town, South Africa, in 1967 – the first human heart transplant.

A NEW ERA

Chief surgeon for this historic operation was Christiaán Barnard (born 1922). Technically it was not a very demanding or difficult procedure. Its importance lay in the old idea that if the heart stopped, the body was dead. But medical technology had moved on. In 1966 French doctors were first to use the idea of brain inactivity, rather than a stopped heart, as the main sign of death.

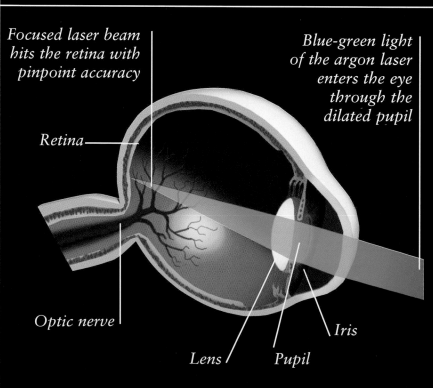

26

LASER EYE SURGERY

Focused laser beam hits the retina with pinpoint accuracy

Blue-green light of the argon laser enters the eye through the dilated pupil

Retina

Optic nerve

Lens

Pupil

Iris

One of the first practical uses of laser light was eye surgery, from 1962. A ruby laser beam could be directed accurately to cut just a tiny area with its intense heat, leaving nearby tissues undamaged. The beam came to a concentrated point or focus inside the eye so that it passed through the outer layers without harming them and carried out its work at a precise depth. The beam's heat also 'welded' blood vessels closed as it passed, so there was less bleeding than with a scalpel incision. The laser can 'spot-weld' a loose or detached retina (light-sensitive layer) back to the inside of the eyeball. In 1965, Francis L'Esperance argued that the blue-green light of an argon laser would be more effective than a ruby laser. In 1968, he treated his first human patient with an argon laser.

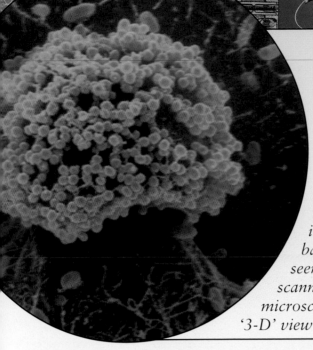

The electron microscope could see much smaller items than the light microscope.

These small blobs are individual bacterial germs, seen through a scanning electron microscope. It gives a '3-D' view with depth.

SEEING SMALLER

Electron microscopes use beams of electron particles to see much tinier objects than with an ordinary light microscope. In 1969 the first scanning electron microscopes were developed. Instead of looking through a tiny object or very thin slice, as in other microscopes, the electron beam scans to and fro across its surface. This provides a more realistic three-dimensional view.

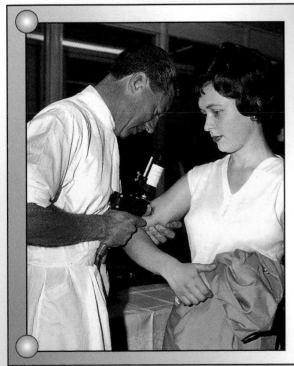

MORE VACCINES

After the success of a vaccine to immunize, or protect, the body against polio, more vaccines were introduced in the 1960s. They included measles in 1965 and rubella (german measles) in 1969. However a few people fell ill after vaccination. New guidelines were introduced so that people who had certain conditions, or a family history of these conditions, did not receive the vaccine.

Vaccine by injection.

HAVE AND HAVE-NOT

After tests in the late 1950s, the contraceptive pill became generally available in the early 1960s. It altered the female hormonal cycle to prevent conceiving a baby. In 1967 another hormone-based pill was introduced to do the opposite. The 'fertility drug' clomiphene encouraged the female body to produce more ripe eggs, increasing the chances of having a baby.

GADGETS

Most types of electrical appliances designed to take the hard work out of chores, such as washing machines and vacuum cleaners, were well established by the 1960s. The new generation of gadgets was more to do with convenience, entertainment, leisure and just plain fun.

The skateboard craze began in 1962 with boards rolling on ball-bearing wheels made of new, soft but tough rubber. No longer did you need sea to 'surf'.

FAST FASHION

Shrinking electronics, smaller batteries, plastics, and new methods of mass production made for a whole range of smaller, more portable, hand-held devices. They included radios, tape players, TVs, clocks and cameras. They were designed to look bright, work quickly, and be simple to operate.

Telephone buttons (1963) worked faster than the usual rotary dial.

TIME FOR ACCURACY

A quartz wristwatch is based on a crystal of quartz (silicon dioxide) – the same mineral that forms sand grains. An electric current passed through the crystal makes it oscillate or vibrate exactly 32,768 times each second. A microchip counts the vibrations and produces regular pulses of electricity that turn the rotor, and via gears, the watch hands.

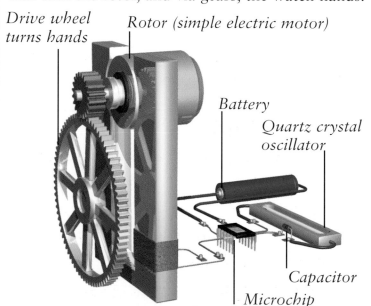

Drive wheel turns hands

Rotor (simple electric motor)

Battery

Quartz crystal oscillator

Capacitor

Microchip

SMALL MUSIC

Large reels of magnetic tape were used by professionals to record and play music. In 1963, Dutch company Philips made a small version for everyday use. The tape reels were protected inside a little case or 'case-ette'. Unlike vinyl discs, you could record as well as play. This new sound medium was also more convenient than discs and less affected by movement.

Cassette tape was too narrow (6 mm) and moved too slowly past the record/playback head to produce high-quality sound. But it was very easy to use and handy to carry.

The Kodak Instamatic 50 (1960) turned everyone into a photographer.

HAPPY SNAPS

'Convenience' and 'ease of use' were the new key terms. Consumer gadgets seemed simple, but this masked sophisticated design and advanced technology. For example, anyone could take snapshots with the Kodak Instamatic. The photos might not be quite up to professional standards but were good enough for most people. The camera had a new lens design and advances in film chemicals allowed just two settings, sun and cloud!

THE FINAL WORD

The 1960s saw many other convenience inventions such as ring-pull fizzy drink cans, the electric toothbrush and the artificial grass Astroturf, first used in the US's Houston Astrodome. It seemed that science and technology could solve any problem. But in the next decade, the 1970s, the effects began to appear as pollution and other environmental problems.

Nib and ball-point pens had hard, unyielding tips. Felt- and fibre-tip pens were softer and easier to control.

GLOSSARY

ANNEALING LEHR In metal- or glass-making, an oven-like area where the product is heated and then cooled precisely to make it harder and tougher.

ATOM The smallest part of a pure substance (chemical element) that can exist naturally. Most atoms are made of three types of even tinier particles called protons, neutrons and electrons.

INTEGRATED CIRCUIT A small device which contains many electronic components, such as transistors, resistors and capacitors, already linked or integrated into whole pathways or circuits.

LASER A device that produces waves of intense, powerful, high-energy, pure-colour light. The term stands for Light Amplification by Stimulated Emission of Radiation.

MASS PRODUCTION The manufacture of standardized products in large quantities, usually by machines.

PALEOMAGNETISM Scientific study of the Earth's natural magnetic field during prehistory, especially from tiny magnetized particles trapped in ancient rocks.

POLYMER A substance whose molecules (chemical building parts) are made of identical units, monomers, joined like beads in a necklace or bricks in a wall.

PULSAR A relatively small, amazingly heavy or dense star that gives off pulses of energy. It is probably a fast-spinning neutron star left over from the explosion of a giant star.

QUARK One of the smallest pieces of matter, an elementary or fundamental particle. Quarks of various types and combinations make up slightly larger particles such as protons and neutrons, which in turn are parts of atoms.

QUASAR A region of space which gives off more energy than almost any other. It perhaps consists of an entire galaxy falling into a giant black hole.

SPACE PROBE An unmanned craft that travels into space, usually to fly near or land on another planet, a moon or, in the case of Giotto, a comet.

UNITARY (MODULAR) CONSTRUCTION When a structure is built from many similar parts, units or modules.

30

TIMELINE

	SCIENCE EVENTS	TECHNOLOGY	FAMOUS SCIENTISTS	INVENTIONS
60	•International agreement on defining the metre by the wavelength of a certain kind of light	•First submarine-launched Polaris nuclear missiles •US X-15 rocket plane sets air speed record	•Rudolf Mossbauer discovers the gamma ray effect named after him	•First laser built by Theodore Maiman •Last British tram (trams reappear in the '90s)
61	•Yuri Gagarin becomes first person in space •Chaos theory is firmly established	•Cuss I drilling rig bores 185 m into the ocean floor to reach the basalt bedrock of the ocean crust	•Louis and Mary Leakey find fossils of the earliest human, Homo habilis, in East Africa	•Electric toothbrush •Barnett Ventilator, a medical electric lung pump
62	•Telstar 1 sends on, or relays, live TV broadcast •A new particle group, hadrons, identified	•US nuclear-powered cargo ship Savannah begins sea trials	•Rachel Carson's book Silent Spring makes people aware of chemical pollution in nature	•First commercial skateboards go on sale •First industrial robots installed by Unimation, US
63	•Syncom 2 is first satellite in geosynchronous orbit, staying over same place on Earth	•First satellite launched to study X-rays from space	•Giulo Natta and Karl Ziegler receive Nobel Prize for work on polymer plastics	•Audio minicassette •Friction welding •Measles vaccine
64	•US Ranger probe sends back 4,300 close-up photos of the Moon	•Verrazano Narrows Bridge, New York, takes record for longest span	•Murray Gell-Mann writes his major account of quarks	•MTST becomes first word processor •Stay-pressed non-iron clothing •Containers for ships
65	•The planet Venus is discovered to spin in the opposite way from other planets	•US spacecraft Gemini 6 and 7 dock in orbit •Automatic landing system for aircraft	•John Kemeny and Thomas Kurtz invent first computer language for beginners, BASIC	•Widespread use of fertility drugs •Early holograms
66	•French Academy of Medicine begins to use brain inactivity as an indication of death	•Fast-breeder type of nuclear reactor developed •Luna X is first probe to orbit the Moon	•Konrad Lorenz's book On Aggression compares origins of animal and human aggression	•Fuel injection for fast cars •Early Dolby system to reduce hiss and noise on tape recordings
67	•First heart transplant by Christiaan Barnard in South Africa •Pulsars discovered	•US Transit system becomes first satellite navigation method	•Arthur Kornberg and team are first to copy DNA in the laboratory	•First colour TV broadcasts in Britain •Mammography for detecting breast cancer
68	•Apollo 8 goes to the Moon, orbits 10 times and returns safely	•USSR's Tupolev Tu-144 beats French-English Concorde as first supersonic jetliner in the air	•Joseph Weber reports first finding of theoretical gravitational waves; not many take him seriously	•First oil-carrying supertankers •Radiation (waves) to sterilize and preserve foods
69	•The world watches on live TV as Neil Armstrong becomes first person on the Moon	•Hurricane Debbie is weakened by 'seeding' with silver iodide crystals	•Jonathan Beckwith and team isolate the first single gene, for breaking down sugar	•Home yogurt-makers •Bubble memory for computers

31

INDEX

32